A Guide for Beginning Indie Authors, Freelance Writers

By

Mike Reuther

http://www.amazon.com/Mike-Reuther/e/B009M5GVUW

Introduction

Right here, in this book, is a gold mine of valuable information for becoming the writer you want to be. There exist plenty of opportunities for writers these days. Unfortunately, too many people who want to see their words published and even make money at writing don't know how to get started.

This book shows the many options for writers, from ebooks, which revolutionized publishing, to the many freelancing markets out there. If you're an aspiring novelist, you'll find publishing and writing advice, even inspiration and best strategies for creating a book. Authors and other experienced writers can come away learning a few things from this book as well.

Much of what is in this book can be found in my other books on writing. Here, it has been put together in one comprehensive format. This book was first published in 2015 but has been updated.

If you're like many writers, you are perhaps exploring different markets for writing. I hope you find this book helpful, and it serves as a guide for your writing journey.

Ready to get started?

Let's go.

Write an Ebook

Chapter 1

What book do you want to write? A mainstream novel? A mystery? A western? Maybe you have the latest and greatest diet and fitness regimen you want to release to the world and would love to describe it all in a book. Politics, health, history, the paranormal, your life story. You can write about anything. Write to your heart's desire. There's no publisher or agent to reject you. As an ebook author, you can truly write the book of your dreams.

So what's stopping you?

Only you can decide if you are ready to write a book. Don't expect to get rich writing an ebook. The fact is a lot of people are writing them these days. Perhaps no one in your orbit of friends or none of your co-workers is a writer. But rest assured, plenty of folks are out there scribbling away on paper or banging away on keyboards. And why not? The ebook revolution has ushered forth marvelous opportunities for writers. Don't get me wrong. It's great that the door has swung wide open for writers. But with so many ebooks flooding the marketplace, it's quite hard to make your own stand out from the pack.

Marketing is important. No mistake about it. Plenty of information can be found about how to best market your ebook. Quite frankly, I don't know the single best marketing strategy. I don't know if anyone really does. You can blog until your fingers bleed; you can tap into Facebook and do Twitter. You can do podcasts, go on the radio and gab about your book. Some authors hire publicists. Of course, there's the good old-fashioned word of mouth that will always bring you a few readers as well.

I've done them all, save hiring a publicist which can be beyond the budgets of many authors. Stories vary as to how effective a publicist can be in helping an author launch and promote a book. Of course, publicists can save you the time of doing the marketing yourself. And let's face it. For most authors, time is what many of us would much rather use to spend writing. If you decide to hire a publicist, take your time to look around and find a good one. Learn exactly what the publicist you're thinking about hiring can do for you. Will the publicist perform the marketing itself or merely advise you what to do? Query other writers. Find out if publicists have helped them.

Many authors who publish their books through Amazon sign up for the company's KDP Select program which offers authors the option of offering their books free up to five days during any ninety-day period. Here's how it works. Say your ebook, *The 1001 Ways to Sell Junk at Yard Sales* regularly is priced at $2.99, but you've had problems selling it. To draw more attention to it, you decide to offer it for free for three days, and after those three days you are thrilled to see that it generated 603 free downloads.

Now what? The hope is that you've drawn sufficient attention to your nifty little book on yard sale success, and readers who didn't take advantage of the free offer will now go ahead and buy it at its regular $2.99 price. Alas, 603 downloads are not a lot. You'll be lucky to get more than a couple of sales as a result of your free offer.

I've made use of the Amazon KDP Select free option, with just modest success. In fact, the most number of free downloads I ever managed was for my murder mystery, *Return to Dead City*. In April 2014, the book grabbed 3,657 free downloads. I subsequently made about 10 sales or so of my book shortly after the free download period ended.

Some of the other books I offered for free through the Amazon KDP Select free option during 2014 fared as follows:

•*Gambling Lives*, 602 downloads, five days.

•*The Crazy Writers Group*, 29 downloads, two days.

•*Write the Darn Book*, 500 downloads, five days.

•*Nothing Down*, 372 downloads, three days.

•*Return to Dead City*, 3,657 downloads, three days.

•*Baseball Dreams, Fishing Magic*, 107 downloads, two days.

That's not to say I regret having tried this fee option different times. It has given me, a relatively unknown author who only started publishing less than ten years ago, a chance to have my books recognized and read by people. The program comes at no cost. Over the long haul, offering my books for free at selected times has been a good move. At the same time, it's important that I continue to write and publish more books.

There was a time when authors did quite well with KDP Select's free program. Authors who saw their books downloaded more than ten thousand times were not unheard of. But in recent years, for whatever reason, perhaps the ever-increasing flood of books coming on the market, the KDP free option doesn't yield the downloads it once did. The fact that so many ebooks are cheaply priced to start with perhaps has much to do with this as well.

My advice to new authors is to give the KDP Select free option a chance. It can't hurt, and it can get your books noticed. Who knows?

You might be one of those lucky authors to receive ten thousand or more downloads, giving your book the kind of jump-start that leads to many sales. Just don't depend on it for all your marketing.

Keep in mind also that KDP has in place an exclusivity clause, whereby authors cannot have their books with any other publisher but Kindle. You can read more about that a little later in this book.

Of course, you can spend money on sites such as ReadCheaply to advertise your free download days. Many other sites charge authors nothing to advertise their free days. However, some of those sites offer no guarantees that they will even run your promotions. Should you pay to promote a free book? Only you can decide that or how much you are willing to spend for any kind of advertising.

KDP Select also offers the Kindle Countdown Deal to allow authors the option of discounting prices of their books for up to five days during any 90-day period.

Try some of the different marketing strategies. Experiment. You can spend a lot of time and money marketing. Of course, you don't want to give up time that can be better spent writing your next book.

Mark Dawson was a struggling author who found a vast network of readers through email marketing. Many other authors have used his strategies to find their own readers and sell books.

I've found the use of Amazon Ads to sell many my fiction and nonfiction books. The ads are rather easy to set up and work through the process of using keywords that readers use to find books on the Amazon network.

There are plenty of tutorials online out there on email marketing and Amazon Ads. Check them out.

Get to know some other writers in the vast independent authors community. Many are just starting out as writers and struggling to get their books before readers. Find out what's working for them and what isn't.

Consider joining a local writers' group in your community. It's a chance for some face-to-face contact with other authors who can offer advice, counsel and even friendship. In many of these groups authors exchange ideas and read each other's books. Chances are someone in the group has been successful with epublishing. Find out what others are doing and not doing. Writing and marketing can be a lonely, even frustrating process, and it's good to be around people who have been through some of the same experiences as you. Writers' groups are everywhere. Check the internet or your local library to find one that meets near you. Plenty of writing groups can also be found online.

Print up business cards with your book and contact information. Let people know you've written a book. Urge them to read it. A little self-promotion doesn't hurt and can multiply with just one person. Let people know you're an author.

Get reviews for your book. There's no question that many readers look at a book's reviews before deciding to purchase it. Without exception I always read reviews of a particular book before making a buying decision. The more reviews a book receives, the more likely I am to think that it might be a book worth reading. It's just human nature.

You might well be thinking: But what if I solicit reviews for my book and I get nothing but negative feedback? Fear not. That's not likely to happen, unless, of course, you write a horrible book. Not everyone will like your book. I don't care how good it is. Secondly, a little criticism is usually better than no review at all. Get reviews for your book. It shows people are reading it.

Now, where do you find reviewers? Some of the best places for finding them are on the Amazon pages. Some Amazon reviewers have a little more clout than others. Hall of Fame Reviewers with Amazon, for example, have attained special status. Ideally, those are the reviewers you want to consider your books. Convincing them to review a book isn't always easy, however. Often, they have a backload of books to read. But Amazon has tons of other people reviewing books as well. Anyone can review books or other products sold through Amazon. To track down one for your book, check out some of the books like yours on Amazon. Find out who reviewed the books. Click on the reviewer's name and jot down the reviewer's contact information. Send the reviewer a short message asking for a review of your book. You may only find a couple of people willing to review a book for every twenty requests you send out, but don't get discouraged.

There are plenty of other places to go for reviews. What about your local newspaper? Many newspapers have freelancers or at least someone on staff who reviews books, but many online sites can be found for reviewing books. Keep in mind, some book review sites charge writers in exchange for reviews. Some can be pricey.

I once tried a little different approach to find reviews for one of my books. I signed on with a promotional company to spread the word about my novel to various media outlets. I managed to receive a few reviews, but for the price I paid it didn't seem worth it. Plenty of people review books at no cost. Get on Facebook and other social media sites and look around.

Some authors opt to do book review exchanges with other writers. I don't know how many times I've been contacted by email or through Facebook by an author to read his or her book and give it a review, in exchange for that writer doing the same for one of my books. This can be dicey. I'm not a big advocate of book review exchanges. In fact, I no longer do them.

Many authors expect to receive at least a four-star review for their book. What if the book is horrible? Can you be brutally honest reviewing someone's book at the risk of perhaps receiving a bad review for your book from that same author whose work you ripped? Of course, you want a favorable review. We all do. Amazon frowns on book review exchanges. It is believed that Amazon even erases reviews of books that are part of this swapping process.

We'd all like to get *The New York Times Review of Books* or *Publishers Weekly* to review our books. But for independent authors, it's not likely to happen. Kirkus Indie http://kirkusreviews.com/indie/about), reportedly reviews indie books at the hefty price of more than four hundred dollars. Kirkus Indie carries quite a bit of clout in the publishing world, and a review from Kirkus can help an author's book get noticed.

Put your book on as many book-or reader-related sites as you can find. One of the best is Goodreads. At last count, Goodreads had 90 million members and in 2013 was acquired by Amazon. Once you become a member you can list any of your books on Goodreads. It's a free site, and you can list your books on Goodreads as well. The Goodreads Giveaway, a kind of lottery in which readers enter their names to win a copy of an ebook or print version of a book, is popular. Hundreds of readers usually are involved in a single book giveaway, and it's a golden opportunity for authors to get their works noticed and read. Authors can put up multiple copies of their books to be given away. The author is responsible to ship copies of books to the winners. Winning readers are encouraged to review books which can be a real plus for authors. Goodreads includes all sorts of other services as well. You can interact with other authors on the site and connect with readers. Given the incredible popularity of Goodreads, it's a must site for writers.

Shelfari is yet another site for authors to connect with readers. Launched in 2006, it was later acquired by Amazon. Once you get your books on Amazon, they will appear on Shelfari.

Some authors promote their books on YouTube, and it's worth considering. There is no limit to what you can do to advertise a book on this hugely popular site. Include a link of your YouTube book promotion on the various other sites you use to promote your book. There's no telling who will stumble across it.

You might want to make your book available in an audio version. Many people listen to books rather than read them. Those with long commutes to work listen to books being read by a narrator during long drives to their jobs. Vacationers on the road turn to audio books as well. Others simply prefer audio books. You can hire someone to narrate your book, or you can do the talking yourself. The Audio Publishers Association reported $940 million in publisher receipts in 2018 publisher sales data – the seventh years of double-digit sales growth in the U.S.

Chapter 2

You can't judge a book by its cover. Well. That's certainly true. I often think of the cover for one of my favorite books, *The Catcher in the Rye*. One of the old editions of the classic J.D. Salinger novel has a simple red cover with the title and the author's name in yellow letters. The cover really is as bland as that. It doesn't matter. *Catcher in the Rye* has sold millions of copies over the years.

Of course, a book with the universal appeal and literary value of Salinger's novel doesn't need a sparkling or sexy cover to sell it, but most books aren't in that position. The fact is a cover is important in selling a book. Think about this. When you're in a bookstore scanning the shelves, are your eyes likely to stop at some of the titles with the more provocative covers? Perhaps not if you're looking for a particular book. But if you're just browsing, it's quite likely you'll pause, even pick up that book with the attractive cover.

When covers of ebooks come up on Amazon, where do your eyes stop? Covers, whether you like it or not, help sell books. Some argue that a cover is perhaps the most important aspect of an author's marketing strategy.

It's easy for writers to dismiss this aspect of the publishing process. After all, writers put words to paper. They don't have the time to worry about book covers. Let someone else worry about that. Or so the popular notion is for many writers.

Don't fall into that line of thinking.

So, how do you, the author, find a cover for your ebook? The good old internet is a likely place to track down those who design and create covers. For as little cost as five dollars, an author can get a cover done. That's right five dollars. You can also spend upwards of one thousand dollars for a cover. While I can't stress enough the importance of a good cover, I'm not one to tell anyone to spend money they don't have. The fact is you can get a nice cover at a cost that will cover a night out for dinner. Again, check around.

Fiverr.com is a great resource for book covers. The site also includes plenty of other services for writers including editing, book-formatting, and a whole host of other offerings. Graphic artists who contract out their services with Fiverr will work with you to get just the right look for your cover. Check the ones with the five-star ratings. Other sites for book cover designers include www.guru.com and www.elance.com.

You can, of course, design your own cover. The choice is up to you. Again, a good cover is crucial for getting your book noticed and read. Don't dismiss this very important component of your book. A good cover can truly help sell it. Consider getting several covers done. Share them with others and find out what ones they think are best. It's worth taking a little bit of time to decide on the right cover.

Picking a good title is important. It's probably more important for nonfiction books that are about a particular subject. Readers looking for a book about say, how to fix clocks, want to be able to find it, and if you slap on a vague title such as *Time to Rewind* (clever perhaps for a whimsical time travel novel, and you're welcome to steal it if you like), I'm not so sure readers interested in clock repair will find your book. Titles should grab the attention of readers, and that can mean just a few words that convey the message you want to get across. Use power words in your title. Success, money. Those words have power. They get noticed.

But what about Search Engine Optimization? Well, what about it? Books and blogs and podcasts have been devoted to Search Engine Optimization, otherwise known as SEO. There's little question that some books on the internet are more easily found than others. Say you write a book about basic gardening that you want to sell. Chances are the day it's released it won't find its way on page one of Amazon or Google for gardening or book on gardening.

Creating a title that includes the words that readers are more likely to type into search engines to find a book of your genre can certainly push you toward more sales. That goes as well for having the right keywords for the descriptions of your book on your Amazon book and author pages. Search engines pick up on certain words. I'm not sure anyone knows for sure how it all works. Check out some of the books on SEO's. They are loaded with strategies.

Chapter 3

You've poured your heart and soul into your first book. You've finished that very important first draft. You're ready to start editing and polishing it and getting it ready for publication. Ideally, you used a good computer program with a spell check to write your book. You spend a few days reading through the manuscript, finding mistakes, correcting them. Perhaps you change some scenes or information in the books, strike out extraneous material. Now what?

Consider hiring an editor. Maybe you know someone who's willing to read through your book and offer criticism and look for mistakes. Perhaps you know a few people who can provide this service. This isn't the time to shrink from criticism, to be afraid someone might not like your book. Not everyone is going to do jump with joy over your book and declare it the greatest work of the Twenty-First Century. You'll understand this perhaps more clearly once you begin publishing and receive reviews on Amazon and other sites. But I'm getting ahead of myself.

Hand off your book to a professional who can give it a good editing. A second set of eyes or more looking at your book can only help. You certainly don't have to do everything to your book an editor suggests. As a matter of fact, you don't have to change anything. But you might be surprised what suggestions an editor comes up with. An editor can often improve a book. Just having someone to pick up on those nagging problems of syntax and grammar can be a big help. Check out www.elance.com, a good site for finding an editor or proofreader.

Some independent authors sign on with beta readers. Beta readers can be friends, fellow authors, interested readers who look at your book. You might be surprised of the number of people out there who love to read books and even help authors.

Chapter 4

When I finally published my mystery, *Reader to Dead City*, as an ebook, I went with Smashwords, a publishing company for independent authors started by Mark Coker. Coker is an author who tried for years without success to be published. The company has done quite well, with a catalog of more than 500,000 books at last count. Smashwords includes a primer new authors can download that takes them through the steps of publishing their books as well as strategies for marketing it and designing it.

To get your book noticed, it's a good idea to make it available as widely as possible. Amazon remains easily the biggest sales platform for books, but you're missing out on additional exposure and all-important sales if you ignore Smashwords, Draft2Digital, Lightning Source and other publishers that distribute to various sales channels.

What you want to write about is up to you. The ebook world publishes all genres of books   mysteries, westerns, romances, memoirs, histories, biographies. You name it. Maybe you've always wanted to get all those wonderful recipes into a book for others to read. Perhaps you're working on a family history. Go for it.

Hopefully, you have time five or six times a week to write your book. Or maybe you don't have that kind of time. Many people want to be writers but simply have too many other responsibilities and activities in their lives – work, piano lessons, running kids to ball games, attending meetings. They can't imagine allotting even a few minutes a day to write.

It all comes down to priorities. How long have you wanted to write? A long time? Have ideas for books been swirling in your brain to the point that you simply burn with a desire to write a book? If you answered yes to either or both questions, perhaps it's time to get started on that ebook. Remember, there's really no better time to be an author than now and getting your work out there to readers is well within your reach if you're willing to just take the time to do it.

Set up a writing schedule. Pick ninety minutes to a couple of hours a day, five or six times a week and start writing. Most of us need to get into the rhythm of writing nearly every day. It's part of the writing process, the momentum of putting down words. However, if you can only write once or twice a week, by all means at least do that. Any writing is worth doing, and you may find once you get started that you can squeeze in other minutes of the week from your busy schedule to write.

Maybe you're intimidated about writing a book, or at least something lengthy. The idea of pounding out say, fifty-thousand words, to tell a story seems an insurmountable task. Epublishing does not discriminate against short story writers, authors of short books.

A flood of books can be found on Amazon that are no more than twenty or thirty pages. Some are even shorter. This book you're reading isn't terribly long. Maybe that's why you decided to download it. Plenty of readers are looking for quick reads, and that's good news for authors, especially those who want to write a series of books on a single subject or on any number of topics.

How about you? Maybe you're an expert in some field – woodworking, masonry, ham radio – and you have all sorts of ideas for books. Consider writing a series. Of course, you can write a single book about a subject and be done with it. Everyone is looking for information of some kind, and you may be just the person to write the book on a subject that many readers want and need. A subject may have been written to death, but that doesn't necessarily mean you decide against writing a book about it. As an author, you can always add your own unique voice, your own perspective to any topic.

Maybe you've been a successful fast-food franchise owner with a yen to write a book about everything you know about the subject. Whatever topic you choose for a book you should make sure you *want* to write about it. It's even better if you have a real passion for the subject. Choose to write about things you don't really care about, and it's likely to become a chore once you sit down and start tapping on the keyboard. And guess what? It will show in your writing. The same goes for fiction. If you're writing a novel, make sure it's a story you want to tell.

Writing should be fun, not drudgery. Oh sure. You're not always going to be happy while writing. And there will be a lot of days when it will be hard to get started. The start to any endeavor is often the hardest time, no matter what it is. Just remember, the first step is just the beginning.

Don't Fool Around, Write Fast

Chapter 5

When I sat down more than thirty years ago to write my first book, I resigned myself to the idea that it was going to take me a long time to finish it. I figured to be writing and stopping and trying to figure out where my story was really going as I got into the creative process. I mean, that's just the way an author went about writing books. Writing, I figured, was an arduous task, not an endeavor to be entered into lightly. In essence, writing took work and that meant countless days of stringing together words.

Sure. I had heard there were these creative geniuses who banged out books in no time at all. These were strange creatures, of course, like those crazy artists who threw paint at canvasses. Rare birds indeed, blessed with an ability to spit out their thoughts onto paper in rapid fashion as if they were Robin Williams going off on a comedic monologue.

Writing a book, I concluded, would take discipline and planning and plenty of left-brain thinking. I wrote my first few books slowly, in this deliberate sort of fashion. I was a part-time novelist with a day job as a newspaper reporter. You might say I had some bad habits to break. Writing about current events and community news required me to collect facts, mull them over in my brain, and get my ducks in a row before putting together my articles.

Learning to write fast was basically unlearning everything about writing I knew. Perhaps if I had early on been published, I would have kept on with this slow writing process. There would have been no reason to change this approach. This was in the days when it was quite difficult to be a published author. Authors wrote books and then hoped some literary agent would find them a publisher who would pay them a nice tidy sum for their efforts. Epublishing didn't exist. Like many writers, I felt my manuscript had to be beyond perfect before it was looked at by agents and publishers. And so, I toiled at my books, wring them in this slow plodding manner.

A wakeup call came to me some years later. I was still an unpublished writer. I had several novels tucked away in drawers, and two agents had both failed to sell my mystery. For too long I had failed to heed the message that writing a book fast was the best method for creating my stories. It took a leap of faith for me to finally try it. And so, one cold December morning, I began madly scribbling out words on these large pieces of blank sketch pads. This followed a week-long process that included some brainstorming of my story and outlining it.

In less than six weeks' time I wrote the first draft of the book. I suppose I was surprised more than anything. I couldn't believe how quickly I could in fact write a full-length novel. But was it any good? Was it largely a lot of scribbling? Did my story make any sense?

When I read through what I had so quickly written out on those sketch pads, I was happy to learn that the story in fact was fine. I indeed had a book, a story that laid the foundation for a completed novel. Sure, there were misspellings and grammatical errors. Certainly, some parts of the book demanded editing, but I had successfully completed the first draft of a book – and in no time at all.

Chapter 6

There was no turning back after that experience. I now write all my books in this stream of consciousness, fast-writing process. I learned from that first effort that fast writing put me in my natural voice as a writer. The words had quite easily tumbled out of me. I wasn't striving to sound like some other writer – a mistake many authors make while writing books.

Too many of us are afraid to even begin books because we feel unsure of ourselves as writers. The comparison game is a trap we all fall prey to. It's human nature to want to be as good as or better than the next person. A surgeon measures himself up against his fellow surgeons. A chef tests his meals against those of other chefs. Ballplayers compare their batting averages against those of teammates and players from opposing teams.

Too many writers are afraid their work isn't good enough, that the words they put to paper will sound awful, silly, juvenile. And so, they adopt this slow-writing process. I was as guilty of this practice as any writer, forever constructing sentences as if I were putting together a jigsaw puzzle, carefully choosing my words, scrambling for the thesaurus when I wanted to insert just the precise word into my story.

Writing fast means moving past your fears as a writer. It's letting loose and saying the hell with the consequences. But here's the secret: There are no consequences.

No consequences? Really?

Let's be realistic. Let's say you sit down one day and just let loose with that story that's been inside of you for so long. Once at the keyboard you pound out thousands of words in several hours of furious writing. The chances are the writing will be good if you allowed the words to just spill out of you, if you wrote naturally, without fear, uninhibited by misspellings and mistakes and the story getting away from you.

But let's say you didn't like what you wrote. So what? What did you really lose? A few hours of your life? What really were the consequences? Taking a chance with writing a book fast is really no risk at all. For most of you who try, it will work out fine. It allows you to tap into the very essence of the story you want to write because it's written in your natural author's voice.

Chapter 7

Once you have the first draft of your story you can move into the editing, the polishing and the revisions that need to be done. Don't make the mistake of editing as you compose the first draft. That's a slow, arduous process, and it stifles the very creativity that you as an author want to tap.

Sure. Plenty of successful authors write at a snail's pace. There's no question that writers who've had their share of best-selling books, who've tasted the sweet nectar of literary stardom, are slow, plodding writers. No one can argue with success.

But too many aspiring authors who dream of writing books do more dreaming than anything else, precisely because they can't begin the process. It's kind of hard to get out of the starting block when one envisions writing a book as this long difficult road. Many of us grind in despair at the very thought of writing anything – a paper for school, even a letter.

We live in an age of emails and tweets and quick bursts of communication. These short greetings and pithy messages that fill up cyberspace twenty-four hours a day are written by people from all walks of life. So many of us are all but addicted to social media and getting off these messages to friends, acquaintances, co-workers and even strangers. Think about when you send off a funny message to someone on Facebook. Did you spend a lot of time composing your words? Probably not. Almost as quickly as the thoughts came into your head you were tapping out the words on the keyboard.

You wrote the message naturally and in your own voice. You didn't spend an inordinate amount of time searching for just the right words. You were in a relaxed mode. Writing, you see, especially during that first draft, is being relaxed and in a comfort zone, letting the words come out, not forcing them. It's writing from the heart, not the brain.

Chapter 8

What story are you dying to write?

It's an important question to answer.

Maybe you have this incredible story to tell about a championship baseball club that overcame all sorts of adversity to emerge as the best team it could be. It could well be you have a memoir in mind, a need to get down on paper all the innermost workings of your troubled past as a means of helping others get past their own problems.

Maybe you're just dying to write about all the funny episodes of the workplace as a means of coping with awful jobs you've had. Or you just want to write for the sake of telling a story – any story. Perhaps it's a riveting mystery/thriller filled with colorful characters and intricate plot twists.

Whatever it is you want to create, you can do it by writing fast, by spilling the words on to paper just as quickly as you can. Never mind that your book will include all sorts of facts and information. You can write a book fast whether it's fiction or nonfiction. Remember. You can always edit and revise your book later. The emphasis is writing the first draft fast in order to lay the foundation for the completed work.

Again, what story are you dying to write? Can you do it with passion? The story you're going to tell should come pouring out, and without that passion, it will be harder to write. Think about it. You don't want to sit down every day and face a story you don't particularly care about. Otherwise, it will be that much harder to write.

Perhaps a number of books are waiting to come out you. Chances are that's the case if you're reading this book. For years, you've thought about all the stories you've wanted to write. If choosing just one story to make into a book is the problem, then your problem is really a very pleasant one.

Now, all you must do is select one of these stories that have been swirling about in your brain.

Chapter 9

Planning a story is nothing more than a two-step process –
brainstorming and outlining. But let me back up. Chances are, if you
want to write a book, you've been writing it for years. What do I
mean by that?

It's a story that's been swirling about inside you for a long time.
You've been considering it, wondering how to tell it, planning it.
What you need to do now is sit your fanny down in a chair and go
through this two-step process.

Brainstorming is nothing more than a random series of thoughts that
come to you when you think of your book. It's likely you've been
doing this all along. Now, it's time to get those thoughts down on
paper.

Grab a pen and some index cards, ideally several hundred of them,
and find a quiet place where you won't be interrupted. Put the index
cards in a pile in front of you and pick up your pen. Now, just
consider your story. What images come to you? What words? Start
jotting down the single words or phrases that occur to you. Don't
write any more than two or three words per index card. This is a
process that must be done fast. Say, you're writing a novel about a
mysterious stranger who enters the lives of townspeople. Who
knows what thoughts that story will inspire when you start
brainstorming? *Killer? Magic? Dark night?* If those are the very
words that call to you, write them down. The point is to do this
exercise, which is so important in the planning of your book, very
quickly.

Brainstorm for a half hour to an hour for at least a day, perhaps a few days. Go through each of the cards after you've compiled at least several hundred random thoughts. What do you feel is important to the story? What did you write down that has nothing to do with your book? By shuffling through those index cards, you should start to feel a story coming alive.

Next, take up the cards and sketch out an outline of your story. How do all these thoughts come together for your book? It's not necessary to outline your book with chapters. Just create a rough outline of your book from beginning to end. Perhaps you have a protagonist intent on finding a killer. Who are the supporting characters and how do they help or hinder his search for the murderer?

I don't suggest going overboard with an outline. Many writers feel they have to know exactly what occurs in each chapter. But really, you don't even need to know how many chapters you'll have in your book. Remember, a rough outline is fine. Once you start writing your first draft in a fast and furious method, you'll find your book taking off in different directions anyway. But that's fine. Trust your instincts. Go with the flow.

Consider how each of the characters play into the story. I like to do actual character sketches at this point. I write down a few sentences about each person – their likes and dislikes and personalities, how they fit into the story. You'll likely have a good idea of the book's major players at this point.

Don't spend weeks planning your book. Work with the index cards no more than a few days. Sketch out your outline and character sketches for a day or two. You may find yourself during this time walking around with all kinds of second thoughts about what to include or not include in your book. Carry around a notebook and jot down any random thoughts you have. The next day, when you again take up the task of outlining your book, insert some of these points into your story.

Don't drive yourself crazy with the character sketches. However, it's important to know a lot about your protagonist and even the other people who play prominent parts in your story. Who exactly is the protagonist? What makes him tick? What is he after in the story and why? What are some of his personal problems, his eccentricities? How does he interact with the other characters? Make your main character come alive.

Once you start writing your book, you can go deeper into the personalities of your characters if you like. You don't need to describe every physical aspect of a character, a mistake many writers make. If you have in your story a gorgeous femme fatale intent on destroying the male protagonist, there's no need to describe her body measurements, every contour of her body. (Sorry guys.) Leave some things up to the imagination of the reader. You can tell a lot about people through their conversations with each other, their gestures.

Make your characters breathe. Don't be afraid to put them in situations where they get hurt, beat up, challenged. Strong characters make stories come alive. Know the people you are writing about and make them interesting.

Be familiar with the setting of your book. Make sure it fits with the story. Often, a setting determines where the story goes. If you place your story in a big city, such as San Francisco, at least some of your characters should reflect that town. Maybe the protagonist is a stranger to the glittering lights of the big city. How does he or she cope in this environment? How does it help or hinder the protagonist in the story?

Don't fret over how exactly your story will play out before you start writing it. Maybe you know the ending and all the intricate plot twists. If you do, that's fine. But if you don't, it's no reason to panic. In fact, it's often best if you don't know how your protagonist will find the killer, or win the girl or guy, or uncover the stolen gems hidden away in the Australian outback. Beyond that, it's not so very important to know many of the other details that lead up to the climax of your book. Too much planning can back writers into corners, destroying the flow of the writing that is so important in putting together a story.

Perhaps you don't want to be bothered with any of this planning. You just want to jump right into the writing. A book can certainly be written with no outline at all. In fact, the first draft can serve as the outline itself. I feel more comfortable with at least a rough outline before I write my books to give me an idea of where I'm going.

Chapter 10

Once you're putting words to paper just as quickly as you can, your story will take off. Granted, you'll have done your brainstorming and your outline and character sketches, but the story will have a way of getting a little away from you, of meandering off on its own. You may discover new characters popping up in the story. This is all fine and dandy. The key is to go with the flow. Allow these events and characters you didn't foresee in the planning of your book to enter into the story.

One of the great wonders in writing fast is how the subconscious takes over. Many words pour out of you. Scenes you never dreamed about emerge. You'll find yourself in a writing zone. This isn't a time to stop and ponder and think how you should proceed. Surrender to it.

How much you write each day is up to you. It's possible to write an entire first draft of a book in a day. That's right – a day. Think about it. It's quite easy to write several thousand words in just an hour's time if you remain true to the task of writing as fast as you possibly can. Keep yourself in that chair in front of the keyboard for eight hours (with occasional breaks to eat, go to the bathroom and stretch your body) and you can easily write fifteen to twenty thousand words. That's a short book. A full day of writing beyond those eight hours can yield an entire book.

Again, writing write as fast as you can is key to the creative process. That's what you do in the first draft   create, write with your right or non-logical, creative side of your brain. It's writing from the heart. Thinking comes later, when you sit down, take all those words you wrote and begin the task of editing and polishing your book.

Most of you won't choose to write a book in a day. But keep in mind it can be done, and it does open the door to other possibilities. Think about it. Break up that single long day of writing into several days. Certainly, three days of fast writing in six-hour bursts can easily yield a first draft.

Writing a book in a weekend is surely a worthy goal. Don't you think? You might well consider picking a cold couple of frigid days in January to write your book, when the snow is piling up outside and you have nothing else to do.

When you write fast, the words pour forth like a waterfall if you stay true to doing it. It's easy, and it can be fun. But the real kick is when you look at the first draft you've written, and you see how the story came out. Sure, work remains with editing and revisions, but the biggest part of writing your book is behind you. The foundation of your story is now in place. Congratulations. You did it.

Chapter 11

It's very easy to make the mistake of finishing your draft and not editing it. I have more than a few manuscripts stuffed away in drawers from years back that I may never got around to revising. You can lose interest in a book after you let it sit idle for too long. You get anxious to move on to the next project. My advice? Try to get right into the editing, the revisions of your book without too much delay.

When you finish that first draft, and you like what you've written, you'll be riding the crest of a wave. You'll likely be excited, energized to get on with the task of improving it, making it even better. It's a good idea to retain that passion, which is so very important in writing a book.

After you've completed your first draft, take a few days first to read through it. I can guarantee you'll find plenty of misspellings and grammatical errors. After all, you wrote the book in a mad sprint. Don't worry about the mistakes. Fix them and move on to the story itself. Make notes of what needs to be changed during this first sweep through the book.

Later, excise scenes that need to be removed. Rewrite in places where it's needed. Are there spots where your story truly meanders off course? Maybe that strange but interesting character that popped up in the middle of the book doesn't really belong in your novel. Don't be afraid to cut anything that simply doesn't belong. Never mind if you think what needs to be taken out is the best writing in the book. Perhaps you can save the material for another book.

Are you having problems with parts of the story? Make special notes in those spots of the manuscript and move on with your editing. Don't think you have to get everything in your book tidied up immediately.

Of course, you want to write the best book you possibly can. But you can also drive yourself crazy in the editing process. Just as you go with your instincts with writing your book, rely on them when you edit. Sure, you can take forever changing scenes and rewriting, but I wouldn't advise it. You'll never get a perfect story, no matter how much you edit.

When you're done with editing, turn your manuscript over to someone else – a friend, an acquaintance, someone in a reading group you may have found online. Let that person go through the book and make suggestions and edit it. Get a few people to look over your book. Don't be afraid to find a professional editor. This can cost some money, but it can be well worth the price to make your book as good as it can be.

You don't, of course, have to make all the changes that others suggest. It's still your story. The point with editing is to pinpoint the problems and fix them if necessary. Nobody but you should be the final judge of your story. Always remember: It's your book, the one that you, the author, created.

Chapter 12

You may well think that the advice I so freely dispense in this book is fine for novels. But what about nonfiction? Guess what? The fast-writing process can work for nonfiction authors as well.

If you're writing a personal memoir or a self-help book in which you rely strictly on your own expertise, memory or experiences, this is a snap. Such books can be even easier to write than a novel. I clearly recall my satisfaction from completing my earliest book on writing, *Write the Darn Book.* I didn't have to interview anyone. I tapped my own experiences as an author to write it. It was written in a quick burst. My fingers raced across the keyboard.

But even if you want to write a biography or other book that requires its share of interviews and research, you can certainly write the first draft quickly. The same brainstorming and outlining described earlier in this book works. You can, of course, have your facts, your research and interviews done prior to writing the book. But that doesn't mean plugging in all the facts and information and checking everything for accuracy while you write your first draft.

It simply means writing as fast as you possibly can and later inserting the required information. The editing and revisions may take a bit more time than with a piece of fiction, but you'll still have that first draft, that very important foundation in place for your book.

I can almost guarantee that once you start the first draft the second guessing will begin. However, it's likely you'll be so caught up in the writing process and how the words are so easily tumbling onto the page that you won't allow those intrusive thoughts to overwhelm you.

The point is to stay in this flow of writing throughout the entire first draft. Whether you chose to write a book in a weekend or take several weeks, the rhythm and momentum of writing your story will be with you. It's all a matter of keeping the faith which will be easy to embrace once you get started and don't waver from the writing process.

Chapter 13

Are you still unsure if the fast-writing process is right for you? Okay. It's time for a little exercise. Don't worry. It's easy.

Go to your keyboard or grab a pen and some paper (make it several pieces of paper) and take a few moments to reflect on something. It can be just about anything – your childhood, your job, a recent strange incident in your life. Maybe a vacation you took to Paris enraptured you. The sights and sounds of the city were pure delight. Perhaps there's a painful time from your past that's been hounding you of late. Are you suddenly in love? Whatever it is, concentrate for a few minutes or so on these thoughts, these strong images or profound feelings that move you.

Then, just start writing about whatever it is you're thinking. Don't pause; don't stop to consider how best to express your thoughts. Just go with the first images and ideas that come into your brain. Write as fast as you can. Let everything just tumble onto the page. Write for as long as you want.

When you're done writing, put it aside. Later in the day, perhaps the next day, read through it. Do you like what you wrote? Never mind the misspellings and the grammatical errors. Are you surprised how the words seem to flow and seem so natural? If not, you might have failed to follow my instructions to simply write as quickly as you possibly could. I can't emphasize enough how important it is to write fast, without hesitation. You're looking to find your natural voice as a writer. When you write without stopping to think, that's precisely what happens.

Maybe you're a slow typist. If so, writing the first draft in longhand is likely your best approach. I used to scribble out my drafts with a pen. Unfortunately, my penmanship is bad. I tend to write small, and my chicken scratches were sometimes hard for me to read. It made the editing process all that much more difficult.

The choice of typing or writing your first draft in longhand is up to you. Some writers complain of their hands getting tired while writing non-stop in longhand. Initially, this can certainly be a problem. However, over time many writers can eventually overcome those minor aches. It's kind of like adapting to a new exercise regimen.

I like to spend about ninety minutes to two hours a day banging out my first drafts on a computer. Normally, I don't take a break at all during this writing. If you choose to write longer than that, you may well need to stop for a few moments now and then. Keep in mind, however, that the longer you take yourself away from your writing, the harder it can be to once again find that rhythm, that flow.

That goes for missing days of writing as well. Ideally, you should be writing the first draft in successive days. If you take several weeks to write your book, try to write at least five days a week. Six days a week is ideal. However, it's important to take a day off from the writing each week to recharge the creative process.

If you choose to write your first draft in just two or three days, you'll likely need to step away from the keyboard or writing pad occasionally just to take care of the necessary aspects of daily living – to eat, take bathroom breaks and sleep.

Try to write the same time every day which can be so important in establishing that all-important rhythm to your writing. I like to write in the morning before the distractions of the day invade. In the mornings, my mind tends to be fresh and alive. Whenever you choose to write, make sure you allot yourself sufficient time. Ideally, you should find a quiet place for writing, closed off from any potential distractions.

Don't treat your writing like a hobby. Make it a priority in your life.

Chapter 14

Let's say you've embraced the fast-writing process. You're several days into the creation of your first draft. You've amazed yourself and perhaps your friends and others with the news that you've banged out fifteen thousand words, a pace that puts you about one third through the writing of your novel. You're pretty darn excited about it all.

Still, those doubts are creeping in. When you're not writing, all sorts of random thoughts jump into your brain. Perhaps that mysterious stranger that popped into your story early in the book keeps calling you. Maybe he deserves a more prominent place in your story. You're not sure who the killer really is in your riveting mystery/thriller.

Don't be afraid to jot down some of these doubts, these stray thoughts that call to you. But don't rush back to the keyboard to insert them into that first draft you're banging out. Keep them separate. Save them. If you're composing your book in longhand, you can jot these ideas down in the margins of your draft when you're done writing for the day. The point is to stay into the rhythm of your writing in that important first draft.

Certainly, some writers edit as they compose their first drafts. They wouldn't consider not editing as they write. Perhaps you've tried to write a book and found yourself simultaneously editing it. Chances are you found the process counter-productive to creativity, and you never finished that first draft. Get into the flow of your writing. Don't edit as you write. You'll quickly establish that very important foundation for your book.

Are you convinced yet?

If not, try that little exercise earlier described in this book. Better yet, start writing your first draft. And please, ignore those nagging doubts, the ones telling you that you can't write a book fast. You *can* write a book fast. It's really quite easy, but it takes a leap of faith to make it happen.

The detractors may let you know in no uncertain terms that you are doing it all wrong. Don't listen to those naysayers. Listen to those who think it's great that you're writing a book. At least a few people will tell you they wished they had the time, the energy, the commitment, even the talent to do what you're doing.

Don't be afraid to let people know you're writing book.

Make your spouse and family members aware you need to remain uninterrupted when doing your work, especially when writing that first draft. You'll be in a zone during this fast-writing time. The words will tumble out of you, and interruptions can only take you out of that zone.

Chapter 15

I could go on endlessly about the merits of fast writing, how it helps a writer best get into the flow of the story. I believe writers should embrace the process if for no other reason than they can get that first draft done as quickly as possible. It provides the real jumpstart needed to go on and complete a book.

Think about it. You can write a book in a matter of weeks, if not a few days, and move on to your next project. If you really want to be a writer you probably have all sorts of stories flooding your brain, and you likely want to start writing them. Why spend many months, even years on a single book? Granted, some writers do. Some authors spend oodles of time outlining and researching and planning to death a book. Yes, that strategy can work, and I can't really argue with successful authors who take this approach.

Then again, it's likely many of you who chose to read this book failed in earlier attempts to write your own book. You read a lot of books about writing, perhaps learned from well-meaning teachers, or writing instructors that a book must be carefully considered and planned before one even begins to string together words. Perhaps some of you are hoping to find that muse that taps your creativity.

There's really nothing mysterious about writing. It amounts to going to that blank piece of paper or that keyboard and just letting the words flow. That's really what the muse is all about. That strange creature who some believe comes to us at unexpected times to infuse us with creativity doesn't exist. You are your own muse, a person with this amazing ability to create.

As soon as you start writing, you're creating. When you surrender to fast writing, this creativity bursts forth. This is the real magic that happens. When you first experience it, it will surely surprise you, but also inspire you to keep writing.

Everyone has within them this creative power.

But aren't some of us more creative than others? Maybe. Then again, how do you measure creativity? Some of us certainly have learned to harness our creative powers better than others. But why spend eternity thinking you're not creative or without the innate abilities to write a book? If you want to do it, make it happen. Sit down and let the words come out.

Don't worry about what readers will like. Write what you have to say. Write from your heart, your soul. Tell the story you *want* to tell or *must* tell.

Writing Fiction

Chapter 16

If you want to write a novel, what's stopping you?

Really? What's stopping you?

To tell you the truth, it's one of the easiest things to do.

I know what you're thinking. How can this guy say that? I mean, I've wanted to write the book of my dreams for a long time, and he's saying I can easily do it.

Well … you can.

But if you're like many people, you're getting hung up on those nagging questions: How should I start my book? Is it worth writing? Will anyone ever read it? And I suppose these are all legitimate questions. I had some of these same feelings when I started out with dreams of writing my novels and even well after I began banging out stories.

Writing fiction is reaching into your soul and telling the story you want to tell. It's writing that mystery, that romance novel, that western that you've longed to share with the world.

No one is forcing you to write. It's not a job, where you're expected to be at your desk or cubicle or behind the wheel of a truck at an appointed time to perform a certain amount of work. No one is paying you to write a book. You don't have to do it. For many of us, that's a big reason it's so hard to write a book. You simply don't have to do it.

There's no guarantee you'll make any money writing a book. In fact, it's highly likely you'll make hardly any money at all. At least, that is, if you don't try and market it. Of course, in this new era of ebook publishing, you can at least get your work out there before readers with little problem at all. But again, with no assurance of a great monetary reward awaiting you, it's easy to forget about this whole crazy notion of writing a book.

Why should anyone invest any time at all into writing a book, let alone a novel? That's a very good question. You don't need to write. No one does. If you want to write a book, you should *burn* with the desire to do it.

Ask yourself the following questions: Are stories forever swirling in your brain? Do you ever read a book and think you could tell a better story than the author? Do you like to put words to paper and see how they look on a page and how the words sound when you read them out loud? Is the written word something you cherish? Are you a voracious reader who loves nothing better than a good tale?

Here's a tip. Those nagging feelings of whether to write a book aren't likely to soon vanish. Believe me, I know. Dismiss those feelings if you like. Chalk them up to silly notions or a middle-aged crisis, of the crazy whims of youth, if you must. But they're real.

Look around you. What do you see? Chances are you have friends, acquaintances, co-workers who don't care a whit about books. Perhaps no one you know has ever wanted to write a book. The world is not particularly kind to the artist, the creative person. Oh sure, we celebrate great works of art, novels such as *Gone with the Wind* and plenty of other stories that have been made into films. But those are exceptions. Most creative works, be they paintings, novels scribbled out by writers, are ignored. Their creators toil in relative anonymity.

Most of us are not encouraged to pursue a life in the arts. Oh, a creative outlet of some kind is fine as a hobby, but it's better to go to college and study business administration or engineering or something practical. You simply won't be able to make a living as a writer. At least, that's the general consensus.

When I was a young guy, I wanted more than anything to write the great American novel. It was a lofty ambition to be sure. But for the longest time I did nothing about trying to realize that dream. Oh, I kind of had a plan, and it went like this: I'd study journalism in college, graduate from school, find a job with a newspaper, work for a few years to sharpen my writing skills, and then get down to the real task of writing fiction. When you're in your mid-twenties with the rest of your life ahead of you, and the passion of youth is burning inside you like a red-hot flame, anything seems possible.

Unfortunately, I needed a wake-up call, as many of us do, before I started writing my first novel. And boy did I get one. The small-town newspaper where I was working not so very happily was sold to a larger company intent on changes. I was let go from my job, fired, along with many other people.

Just like that, I had all this time on my hands. Time to write. On a Thanksgiving night I picked up a pen and opened a notebook to begin the story that had long percolated inside my head for so many years, a coming-of-age novel that I simply had to write. And so, I wrote, carefully scribbling out my words in longhand before later typing my story on an old manual typewriter. This was the late 1980s. Many of us didn't have home computers in those days. In a couple of years, I tried without success to have it published. But of course, it was the usual story of a first-time author being rejected by countless literary agents.

That's the way it used to be. Writers had no choice but to repeatedly send out letters to agents   the gatekeepers to the publishing houses   hoping, praying that one would sign them to contracts and find them those elusive book deals. It was oh so difficult to get published in those days. Traditional publishers rarely took on new authors. As a matter of fact, it continues to be hard for authors to land lucrative publishing deals. Times have changed, of course. With epublishing, writers can now be published quite easily.

But for many years, I was going up against that world, a kind of David taking on Goliath, yet determined to somehow become a published author. I felt deep in my heart that I was meant to be an author. I didn't want to do anything else.

I held a job, raised a family, lived a life not unlike many people, but I still found time to write in my off-hours. There was no guarantee that all the time I spent writing was going to ever pay off. Still, I wrote and dreamed and hoped that somehow, I would be a published author. And it finally happened, many years later, thanks to epublishing and print on demand.

Epublishing and print on demand have opened doors to writer. Now, anyone can write a book and have it out there flashing on Amazon's pages. I'm thankful for these relatively new trends in publishing. They've given me a chance to be published, to finally have my books out there before readers. No longer does traditional publishing control the book world.

What's stopping so many of you from getting started writing that novel? That mystery? That creepy horror story that will make readers forget Stephen King?

Chapter 17

Try to get away from the notion that whatever you wrote won't be good enough. You need to understand that sitting down to write a book takes a degree of faith, a deep belief that your story is worth telling.

What book do you want to write? That's up to you. The popular markets have long been mystery and romance. But that doesn't mean you write for those readers. Hopefully, you write a book you've long dreamed of writing. Trust your instincts and let the words fly.

I've written mysteries, contemporary fiction and also nonfiction books on writing. I like writing fiction because I can let go and tap my creativity. With fiction, there's no limit to the stories you can tell. You don't know what's going to happen when you sit down at the keyboard every day and surrender to the writing process.

Writing that first book is an accomplishment, and for some authors one book is enough. Many first-time authors feel they have nothing more to write about, that the well for ideas and inspiration is now dry. You can stop with one book. But hopefully your first book leads to more stories that are all just bursting to come out.

There is no shortage of subjects and ideas for books. So where do you find them? Some writers carry around notebooks and jot down story ideas that come into their heads. It's not a bad idea. Ideas can come from newspapers and television, the workplace or from simply staring out the window and watching the squirrels. People are an endless resource for stories and the very lifeblood for all fiction. Think of the fascinating and even heroic people you've known, as well as the odd, quirky and even sinister folks who've come into your orbit.

Once you start writing fiction, you'll find yourself getting more attuned to story ideas. You may find it necessary to keep lists for possible stories. Some writers have a pen and some paper beside their beds, and upon awakening from a night's sleep, jot down their dreams. If you really want to write fiction there's no excuse for running out of ideas. The world is a big place, full of intriguing people and places to know about and explore. But you don't have to be a world traveler to write. There are endless happenings right in your own community. Use your imagination. After all, you're a writer. Start thinking like one.

Maybe you don't want to write a novel. Perhaps you want to begin this fiction writing journey with baby steps. The prospect of knocking out a fifty-thousand-word novel may be intimidating. That's understandable. How about a short story? Go for it. You can knock out the first draft of a short story in a day or two with no problem at all. Writing short stories can be a fine way to exercise your fiction writing skills too. Short stories can often lead to novels or novellas.

It could well be that short stories are all you've ever wanted to write. That's fine. Plenty of writers are penning short stories and uploading them into cyberspace. Check out Amazon if you don't believe me. Who knows? You may sell a whole slew of your short stories.

Chapter 18

Have you thought why you want to write fiction?

In my case, I fell in love with reading and fiction back in high school. Devouring some of the classics of American Literature from authors such as John Steinbeck, James T. Farrell and Thomas Wolfe whetted my appetite for wanting to be a writer. Over the years, having worked in journalism and done my share of freelance writing, I still prefer writing fiction over non-fiction writing.

With fiction I don't have to interview anyone for a story. I can sit down at the keyboard, and by simply using my imagination, let the words tumble out. I don't have to pick up the phone or check my story for facts. Now granted, you can write fiction that combines elements of non-fiction. Perhaps you're working on a realistic murder mystery, and you want to ensure you have all the right elements of how police go about investigating a case. Maybe in writing your mystery, you find it necessary to spend time with law enforcement officials or to do tons of research.

Again, I like to write stories that allow me the freedom to go where my imagination takes me. There's nothing like having a story take flight from your soul. And when it's going well and the fingers are racing across the keyboard, it's like other forces are doing the writing. To write fiction is to embrace the very writing process. It's like taking a trip without a care in the world.

Fly to new heights with your own writing dreams. Whether you write longer fiction or short stories, you can find this rhythm and climb aboard the crest of a wave that takes you to places you could never imagine. Do it. Embrace it. Have fun.

Granted, you won't always find yourself in this rapturous zone of writing. It can't always be that good, with the words coming out so effortlessly. There will be no shortage of days where you might have problems getting into the zone. Often, you will second-guess yourself.

When you're not at the keyboard pounding out prose, you'll spend time thinking of writing. It would be nice if we could all shut down the entire creative process when we're not writing and allow our brains to rest. Alas, it doesn't always work that way. You're bound to have apprehensions about your stories and to find yourself wondering if it's all worth it.

Keep writing. See the writing project through to the end. The beauty in composing that first draft quickly is that you won't have a lot of time to second guess yourself. Keep going back to the keyboard five or six times a week. You'll feel good about yourself every day you do write.

Don't worry if you have to cut back the writing from two hours to perhaps one hour on a given day. At least you've done some writing. And if you miss a day, don't beat yourself up too much. Just get back into it the next day. The fact is you probably will miss a day or two now and then, especially when you start out on this marvelous journey of writing fiction.

Don't worry about word counts. Don't think you have to pound out three thousand words each and every day. Concern yourself more with putting in the time at the keyboard.

Anything worth doing in life is going to present its share of obstacles. But guess what? There are far more difficult things to face in life than that blank page staring at you every day. It's not back-breaking physical work. It's not a boss breathing down your neck to get the work done.

Writing fiction is a chance to tell wonderful stories. I can't think of anything more exciting. Can you? Embrace the opportunity. Go with it. Don't look at it as work. Don't worry that what you write won't be good enough. Remember, we are all our worst critics. Bang out that first draft. You might well be surprised how well you told your story.

And that's my little bit of inspiration folks.

Chapter 19

I learned to write working for newspapers, and over the years I toiled alongside people who were perhaps as eager as me to write fiction. Newsrooms are filled with reporters and editors who dream of tossing aside their jobs and penning the great American novel. Instead, they end up in newsrooms with jobs writing and editing stories about subjects they don't always particularly care about.

The routine of the job demands it. Don't get me wrong. Journalism presents endless opportunities for young writers. As reporters, they can learn about the workings of government and the power structure of communities and how the court system works. It's a job that offers up the chance to meet a lot of people and to learn to write concisely and on tight deadlines.

Early on in my journalism career, I worked for a small paper, sometimes writing as many as three stories or more a day. I had to learn how to write fast. Newspapers have those strict deadlines and getting the story in on time is crucial. It was not uncommon to come back from a meeting with just twenty minutes to write a story, have it edited and sent out to be published. I learned I could write good stories on tight deadlines. In fact, some of my best stuff was the result of fast writing.

I spent a lot of nights sitting through long school board meetings, fidgeting, and fighting boredom, wondering what the heck I was going to write about once I got back to the newsroom. Interestingly, I often ended up finding a direction to my news story once I began to furiously bang out words. I was constricted by facts, and I still managed to make the words come pouring out.

Fiction writers aren't constrained by facts. They have the advantage of relying on nothing more than their imaginations. As you can see, there really is no excuse for failing to get down to the task of writing that novel, novella, or even short story of your dreams.

Chapter 20

The notion of the novelist as a hard-drinking, temperamental soul who lives for his art, but dies in poverty, is one that has been with us for centuries. So, who wants to be a writer? Surely, such stereotypes further discourage so many of us from ever wanting to become authors.

If one must write, is it not better to put that talent to more practical purposes? Perhaps. Only you can decide if you want to take the leap into fiction.

I was determined to write fiction. I made time to write during my off hours from newspaper jobs because I simply burned to write novels. Could I have been more productive or successful had I not been doing all that newswriting? Did a day job as a writer constrain my creative side? I can't really answer that question.

Maybe you spend your days writing technical manuals and you can't imagine coming home and writing fiction, even if starting a novel is something you've dreamed about doing since you were in college. Perhaps you hold down some type of non-writing employment, a job so exhausting and demanding that it leaves you no energy to even begin to think of writing.

On the other hand, maybe you have plenty of time to write. The question is how badly do you want to write fiction? Can you set aside a couple of hours a day to write?

Maybe you don't feel you're qualified to write. You never attended college, and you barely got through high school. In your mind, the people who write novels graduated from Harvard or perhaps were born with the sort of brilliant and creative minds that fueled them to become authors.

Creative writing programs have sprung up in colleges over the past few decades. The idea is that students can enroll in courses and learn how to write fiction from educated professors with advanced degrees. It's not a bad concept, I suppose, but why does anyone need a degree in creative writing from say, from the esteemed University of Iowa Writer's Workshop, to write a novel?

Anyone can write a book. I'm not saying everyone has the same innate writing abilities. I'm not even saying anyone can write a *good* book. You may be a wonderful wordsmith who can string together sentences and tell stories that wow readers. Many people with marvelous writing talent don't even try to write books. Look around at the different writers you might have read. All of them are different. As a young man I read a lot of Thomas Wolfe, who wrote these long, poetic and descriptive passages about people and places he'd experienced. Other writers, such as Earnest Hemingway, a former newspaper reporter, wrote more simply, using shorter, concise sentences. Both were powerful writers.

You have your own unique voice as a writer. Don't try to copy anyone else. Be yourself. Let the words flow. Don't fall into the comparison game.

Do what you must do. Start writing and keep writing.

Chapter 21

Freelance writers make, on average, $61,820 annually, at least according to the Bureau of Labor Statistics. Glassdoor pares down that figure just a bit to $42,120 a year.

For people who don't aspire to live in a beach house in Malibu, such earnings can provide a modest if not affluent lifestyle.

One thing is for sure. You *can* make good money as a freelancer.

And yet, there exist those many writers out there who are struggling just to pay the mortgage. The popular notion has long been with us that being a writer means living like a pauper. For every kid who goes off to college dreaming of becoming a writer, there is a parent trying to talk that son or daughter out of such silly notions. It's more prudent for junior to study and learn a real skill that will earn him sufficient money to raise a family, buy a house and be happy. Writing is for dreamers.

Many folks who call themselves freelance writers simply aren't serious about it. Oh, they may write articles now and then for a newspaper or other publications. They may have a real job on the side they dream of tossing aside, but they simply can't make the break.

Many others out there are banging out mysteries, romance books, vampire stories, or what they hope is the next blockbuster novel. Quite a number of these writers are talented, perhaps brilliant storytellers with a burning desire to become successful. And yet, for all their talent, their efforts, the overwhelming urge to make it as writers, too many of them have seen little, if anything in the way of monetary return.

You may be one of these people, frustrated, but eager to turn the page and move on to the next phase of your life, that of becoming a freelance writer. If you've read this far, you likely have some writing skills. Perhaps you're a frustrated or retired novelist. Maybe you're fresh out college with a degree in English or journalism and finding as so many before you that the traditional job market for your skills is a bit thin. Maybe you simply have a talent for writing and a need to put words to paper.

So how do you get started on this freelance writing journey?

Look around you. Who needs your writing? Who are you? What are your interests? I throw out that last question because the very types of things that interest you, that bring about passion, are the best places to go for stories.

Maybe you love sports. There are plenty of markets out there to write about the games that we play. Do some part-time writing or became a stringer covering football, baseball, basketball, lacrosse, or some other sport for the local newspaper. You don't make a lot of money, but it's a great way to get some writing experience and practice your craft. There's business and health care and entertainment and politics. Health care is an exciting and ever-evolving world, from the perspective of new medical treatments to insurance coverage. Just look at all the news in recent years about the Affordable Care Act. As a longtime newspaper reporter, I can assure you that editors are always on the lookout for people who can write on any of these topics.

But newspapers are only one small market. Get on the Internet and use the good old Google search engine and tap in your interest. Check out what writing gigs are out there. There exists a plethora of opportunities. Granted, they include many low-paying freelance jobs, and you may well turn up your nose at some of the earnings. This is understandable. The sad truth is many people simply refuse to pay writers what they are worth. I could go on endlessly about the horribly low wages for writers.

If you have previously tried to earn money as a freelance writer, you know exactly what I'm talking about. Freelance writing internet sites advertise jobs for as little as five dollars an article. It's a pittance. How can anyone live on that kind of money? Well, no one in my social orbit. And yet, if you are just starting out as a freelance writer, and don't have any written pieces with your name on them, one of these low-paying gigs might be your entry level job.

Editors looking to hire freelance writers often want to know what you've written. They need to see your work. And why not? You wouldn't want to hire an inexperienced electrician to fix the wiring in your basement. You don't want a lawyer representing you who's never had a client. The same goes with writing.

What I'm saying is it's fine to take one or two or even several of these low-paying gigs. But unless you are only going into this whole business of freelancing with the idea of making just enough money to buy tickets for a ball game next month, don't get caught up doing too many of these jobs. For one thing, you'll get frustrated beyond belief. You deserve to be paid more than a paltry sum for your writing efforts.

Too many writers are far too willing to be under-paid, and in my mind, exploited for their hard work. If you spend a half day or more on a project, which could include research, interviews, and finally the writing itself, you should expect a fair wage in return for your work. Lawyers, plumbers, therapists are paid well for providing valuable services to clients. But so do freelance writers.

Think of yourself as a professional. That means acting like a professional, doing the job well, meeting deadlines and turning in excellent, well-written copy. And guess what will happen? You'll be rewarded not only monetarily, but with future assignments from these same satisfied clients.

Don't sell yourself short, and don't sell your work short. It's the only way to approach this whole business of freelance writing. And make no mistake about it. It is a business. Treat it like a business, and you'll be successful.

Chapter 22

You may well ask the question: But do I really have what it takes to be a freelance writer? If you recall in the previous chapter, I mentioned persistence and attitude which are surely important attributes. But what about education? Well, what about it?

Perhaps you have a Ph.D. in English or a degree in creative writing. Maybe you have no college at all. To get a job as a staff reporter on a newspaper, a college degree is almost always a prerequisite. But as a freelance writer, you don't need a certain level of education. After all, you call the shots. To find writing jobs you normally need only to have clips or copies of your writings to show prospective clients or editors willing to hire you for jobs. Don't let the idea that you need a lot of education to be a freelance writer. Some of the most successful writers never attended college. The late Pete Hamill, a celebrated former *New York Daily News* columnist and editor, was a high school dropout. Ernest Hemingway never went to college. Nor did John Irving.

Don't let anything hold you back.

Perhaps you're shy, introverted. Many writers aren't exactly the life of the party. It's a big reason many people become writers in the first place. A laid-back or bashful personality need not stop you as a freelance writer. We live in an age of social media and e-mails when communication is less about talking and face-to-face contact. No longer is it necessary to pick up the phone and query an editor or prospective client about a possible job. Of course, a real live conversation continues to be an effective means of communication.

On the other hand, if you're a social butterfly, you may revel in the people you can meet as a freelance writer. The idea of interviewing folks for articles, of sitting down with business people and going over just what kind of copy they'd like you to write about their company or products may fill with you giddiness.

But whether you are the shrinking violet or the social butterfly, it's not a bad idea to get out and meet people. For one thing, as a freelance writer, you'll spend a lot of time writing. That means sequestering yourself away in a room in front of a computer writing your wonderful prose. It can mean a lot of time alone. Let's face it. As human beings we need social contact with others now and then.

Getting out in the public is important, both for your own emotional well-being and your business.

That's right. Your business. Find ways to meet more people. Don't be afraid to join a club or two, hopefully an organization that interests you. There are numerous civic and charitable groups in any community. Ask around, talk to your friends, your spouse or significant other. Link up with people with whom you share a common interest. Whatever group you decide to join, make sure it's one that you'll enjoy. Don't just join a group merely to network.

Clients and potential clients are everywhere. They may be teammates on your softball team, members of your church or synagogue, neighbors down the street. Let people know you're a freelance writer. Print up some business cards with your email and phone number and give them to people you know and meet. The more people who know you're a freelance writer the better chance you'll have to secure clients. Business cards are cheap and easy to print up.

Publish fliers and post them on bulletin boards at post offices, laundromats, libraries, and other public places that see a lot of foot traffic. Websites are yet another option. They can be produced cheaply, or you can spend lots of money on a site that has all the bells and whistles. But don't just get a website up and running and expect the freelance work to come pouring in unless you are ready to invest in one that attracts plenty of traffic. To make your own website stand out, you might consider hiring an expert on website design and marketing.

Advertising is important. But how much of it should you do? To start, business cards, fliers and word of mouth, are probably sufficient. You don't want to spend tons of money on billboards, newspaper ads and other costly forms of advertising at first. Grow your business. Don't make the mistake many business people make of blowing your budget on advertising before you even get started.

How about radio? Many stations have airtime to fill. They need people to interview. Find out if any of your local stations will interview you at no cost. It's a chance to chat about your business. Of course, there are all forms of social media – Twitter, blogs, Instagram, and the popular Facebook. I won't go into the benefits and downfalls of each of these. A lot of it is free. But beware. Too much time spent at the keyboard on social media can be time better spent on writing assignments.

It's important to budget your time. Consider allotting certain hours of the day for writing and other times for what else needs done to support your freelance business. How much time you need to write every day really depends on how much work you have coming in. Many writing projects can be knocked off in an hour or less. Others take longer. Let's say you write for two hours every morning. That still leaves plenty of the rest of the day to make contacts with clients, conduct interviews or do research. You might also want to allot a bit of time each day separate from the actual writing for editing and proofreading your work.

You likely won't have the means to hire an editor or proofreader for your fledgling freelance business. Yet, it's a fine idea to have a second set of eyes to look over your copy. Perhaps a wife, husband or significant other can read over your work. Maybe you can reward their efforts now and then with a night out, a gift. The point is you don't want to hand in work to a client or editor filled with spelling or grammatical errors which can surely doom you for future writing assignments.

Hire an assistant if you can afford one, someone to help with editing, answering phone calls and emails, and marketing. For most beginning freelancers, an assistant simply isn't in their budget. But an assistant is something to consider later, when the assignments pile up and the dollars start flowing in.

Don't miss deadlines. If an editor wants that piece next Wednesday for the religion section of the newspaper, make sure he gets it by then, if not sooner. Don't be late with assignments. Be a writer that editors and clients can trust.

Chapter 23

Bob Bly is perhaps among the most successful freelance writers in America. It's likely you've never heard of Bly, but he's written a number of books on freelance writing and considered an expert in the field. Beyond that, he's made a good living at it. His forte is business copyrighting. Now, most people who consider freelance writing think about doing articles for newspapers, magazines and websites. The real market, Bly says, is business copyrighting. Companies all need promotional materials – brochures, newsletters and flyers   about their products and other aspects of their business they are selling. Businesses offer great opportunities for freelancers, and the good news is that they often pay well.

Look around at the companies, the industries in your own community. Tap into cyberspace. Could some companies benefit from your writing? Most businesses have no person on staff to do such work. They contract out those jobs. Consider white papers, a very lucrative market. White papers are copy used by companies to help sell products, and businesses pay writers good money to put them together.

How about advertising firms in your area? Perhaps they could use someone to write informational materials for clients. Now you may be thinking: Don't I need expertise in web design or other computer skills to even be considered for such work? Certainly, it helps, but you can be hired strictly as a writer. In other words, businesses need people to write their material. That goes for all kinds of writing you do.

Let's talk about photography. Are you good with a camera? Perhaps you've taken a lot of photos over the years. Why not consider writing and shooting pictures for clients. Photos to go with stories can earn you extra dollars for projects.

Maybe you want to supplement your writing with editing or proofreading. Plenty of businesses putting out copy are looking for people to go over written material, to improve it, find mistakes and make it better. Check out some of the markets on the internet looking for editors and proofreaders.

Chapter 24

Let's say you contact a client. Perhaps that editor at the local newspaper is interested in having another person to write bright features about people and exciting new happenings in the community. However, he's hesitant to try you out because you have no written work to show him.

Consider offering to take on an assignment or two for free. You may balk at doing any kind of work for free, and I'm the first to jump up and down and scream about writers being used and exploited for their work. This is the one exception to my rule. This is a chance to show a potential client what you can do, a chance to build up your resume. Take the assignment. Prove that you can do the job. Chances are you'll get more assignments. *Paid* assignments. Then, you can begin exploring other writing projects for more clients.

Do you like movies or books? Offer to write reviews for the newspaper. How about a column? Perhaps you have expertise or great interest in a particular area – fishing, hunting, physical fitness, cooking, computers. The subjects you can write about are too numerous to list.

What about your church or synagogue? Who is churning out the copy for the newsletters the congregation reads every month? Perhaps it's horribly written. Maybe you could lend a hand there. Or how about the newsletters your Rotary Club writes up? Opportunities are everywhere. And remember. Any journey begins with the first step.

Maybe you don't feel your writing skills are quite up to par, but you still have this burning desire to become a freelancer. There are certainly ways to become a better writer. Enroll in a course at your local community college. Check out the numerous writing courses offered online. Better yet, start practicing your craft. Keep a journal.

Write stories about anything. The point is writing is a craft that needs to be honed.

But please. Don't spend forever practicing your craft. Find clients, get hired for jobs. Many newspapers, businesses, organizations are all looking for someone to turn out copy. You'd be surprised who needs a good writer.

Some years ago, I decided writing resumes for people might be a good way to make some extra money. I purchased a course and learned everything I could about this potential market for freelancing. I put an ad in the local newspaper to advertise my services, and before I knew it, I was receiving calls from people to do their resumes.

I don't get rich doing it, but I don't aggressively seek out clients either. I'm busy enough with other writing assignments. Resumes are easy to put together. All clients are different, of course, but there is a basic formula to follow in writing all resumes. You get to meet a lot of people too. Do a good job for someone, and you can get referrals for future clients.

I can't stress enough the importance of always giving your best effort for any assignment. You never know who will sing your praises and lead you to others in need of your services. No one deserves shoddy work, and any freelancer who has any pride in his or work shouldn't consider giving anything less than a good effort. You don't want bad feedback about your work. There's an old saying that one negative experience often outweighs many positive ones. Always give your best effort.

Herb Cohen was a boyhood friend of the longtime TV and radio talk show host Larry King, but that's not why I bring up his name. Cohen wrote a book called *You Can Negotiate Anything*. The title of the books says it all.

The problem is many people don't negotiate at all for anything. They simply accept what is offered. As a freelance writer you can in many instances set your own rates for assignments. Hang out your shingle, advertise your services, and you can decide how much to charge for writing an article, a business letter, a brochure. Of course, you may be very eager, especially just starting out as a freelancer, to grab any assignments you can find. You may be perfectly happy to write an article for pennies. That's understandable and building up your client list and portfolio is important. But don't get stuck in the rut of taking on nothing but cheap assignments. This can lead to nothing but frustration. Don't be afraid to ask for a little more money for any assignment, especially if you feel you're being short-changed.

Many writing projects take time with interviews, research, even traveling. Make it clear to clients that your time is valuable, that they'll get what they pay for if they hire you. Then, follow through with a good product. If a client can't afford you, perhaps it's time to drop that client. You'll gain respect if you stand up for yourself. There's certainly truth in the adage that the squeaky wheel gets the grease.

Communication is so important in life. Always make sure you know precisely what a client wants. Nothing can more easily doom a freelancer's chances for future work than getting assignments wrong. No one wants to work with someone who can't things right and turns in shoddy work.

Chapter 25

So, you've decided to become a freelance writer. You've had it with hawking janitorial supplies door to door. You're eager to renounce once and for all that telemarketing job. You're ready to jump with both feet into this exciting world of freelance writing.

First, take a deep breath. As mentioned early on, freelance writing is not for the faint-hearted. You need to ask yourself some important questions before you leap into a new career.

Of course, the big question is: Are you willing to forgo steady paychecks and depend on yourself and no one else to earn money? It's perhaps the most important question you'll need to answer before you even consider freelancing. What is your financial situation? Are you forever struggling beneath an avalanche of monthly bills? If you've been the sole breadwinner of your family, renouncing the day job to become a freelance writer may not be the best option right now. On the other hand, if you're single and young and living fairly cheaply, freelance writing may not be such a leap. Yes. There are advantages to being young and single.

The good news is you don't need a large amount of money to start doing it. In fact, you don't really need any kind of investment at all. All you need is a computer and a place to write. The only real start-up costs for a freelance writer are the dollars needed for advertising one's services. But is advertising necessary? That really depends on what you're willing to spend. You can certainly start out with the free and cheap advertising – fliers on bulletin boards, business cards, and of course, word of mouth. Maybe you have a good chunk of money in your savings you are perfectly willing to spend for advertising.

I think it's folly to initially spend too much money. Take time to build up your client list, your business. Start slow. Consider doing freelance writing on a part-time basis at first. I wouldn't suggest giving up the day job right away, unless, of course, you have a spouse, a significant other, a well-endowed parent or uncle who is willing to stake you to a career in freelance writing.

Let's face it. You're launching a new career, one without the benefit of a steady and dependable income. You'll be sailing unfamiliar and possibly treacherous waters for a time. On the other hand, you may be a brave soul seemingly unafraid of new challenges. Maybe your motto has always been: *The more the pressure, the better I perform.* Maybe you need that little bit of fear at your back to get into gear. There's no question some people rise to their greatest heights, perform at their highest intensity when faced with some sort of danger. Granted, giving up a job to become a freelance writer may not exactly be a high-wire act, but it does pose its share of perils.

Only you can decide the right time to become a freelance writer. Whether you do it full time or part time is up to you. You may decide not to do it at all. Or you may give it a shot and find it's not for you, that the steady paychecks, the conventional nine-to-five job is best suited for you. And that's fine. There's nothing like experience to find out what road you should ultimately take in life.

Chapter 26

If you've read this far, you know that I champion fast writing. That goes for freelance writing projects as well books. If you're serious about becoming successful as a freelance writer, you'll begin piling up the assignments, and if you don't write fast, you'll get bogged down with work. You need to quickly do projects. Now, I'm certainly not advocating that you knock off assignments at such a furious pace that you turn out crap. What I am saying is you should work fast whenever possible. Then, go back and edit, polish, perhaps rewrite your assignment. The key is to first have a framework for a project, something you can work with.

You can decide how many assignments you do. That that's the beauty of being a freelance writer. You are your own boss. You decide what projects to take on. Maybe you don't need to write that brochure for the local conservation group. The speech you were approached to write for the politician just doesn't fit into your work schedule, but you'd be happy to be considered for future assignments.

Always leave your options open. Keep a good line of communication with your clients. Spread goodwill. Offer to take some of your clients to lunch now and then. In fact, there are times when you'll need to go to lunch just to get away from your desk. As a freelance writer, you'll spend a lot of time by yourself facing that computer screen locked away in a room. Escape the office occasionally and enjoy a bit of the social swirl if for no other reason than your emotional well-being.

Just because you become a freelance writer, don't use it as an excuse to become a hermit. Get outside, exercise and get plenty of sleep. Your career can only benefit from embracing a healthy lifestyle.

What markets should you tap?

That's up to you. Again, look at your interests. Do you have expertise in some area? What is it? Now you may well feel you're not expert at anything. Well, perhaps you're not a Kung Fu master or a top line chef. But my guess is you're pretty good at or knowledgeable about something. Take that interest and go with it. Tap a market. There's a whole world of people out there dying to know more about so many subjects and hobbies and skills and how to get better at them. You can be that writer that spreads some of your knowledge.

Perhaps you're good at karate or know everything there is to know about ballroom dancing. Again, tap into the internet; check the markets for writing for publications on those subjects. Write a column for your local newspaper about your interest, your hobby. Write a blog about it. People are eager for information on any of a multitude of subjects. You can be the writer to convey that information.

Chapter 27

Another market to consider for the freelancer is ebooks. People are eager for information on topics about money and investments and, of course, jobs. Where we work, what jobs we have, how much money we make, will likely always be popular topics for readers. Maybe you've managed people, worked in retailing, assisted in a political campaign. You almost certainly have some degree of knowledge to share. Some successful authors have found niche audiences writing

short ebooks on specialized topics. Some authors write a series of short ebooks targeting a particular subject, branding themselves as experts on the issue. After all, many people have hobbies, but still others are looking to become more proficient at a skill or to learn something. They are hungry for good information.

Increasingly, people have turned to blogs. It's important to create a blog that is not only well-written but well-designed. Eye-catching graphics can boost any blog. It doesn't have to be fancy, and you don't have to be a computer geek to have a successful one. Blogs can make writers money.

Some writers find blogging fun and easy and tapping away on the keyboard on a subject near and dear to your heart and uploading the blog into cyberspace is just about as simple as email. You can gain a network of followers. Blogs can also turn into books. My blogs on becoming an author were used for my book, *How to Write a Book Without Going Crazy*. There's plenty of information out there about successful blog writing. Check it out. Blogging may be your ticket to freelance success.

You don't have to be a great wordsmith to be a freelance writer. Oh sure, it's nice to be able to pour forth prose that dazzles readers. But for a freelance writer putting together articles, business reports and newsletters, getting out accurate information is what's important.

Are you funny? The world could always use more comedy. Take the humorous moments from your life and share them with the world.

Have a great time writing a quirky or funny column or blog. You may gain a host of followers, and who knows where that can lead?

Keep alert about what's going on in the world. If you're not a big reader, become one. Pick up the newspaper now and then and find out what's happening in the world. You may stumble across some ideas for freelance stories. Don't be afraid to try and write about issues you're afraid might bore you to tears. These might be the best markets. During my long newspaper career, I faced many assignments with a feeling of dread, wondering how I was ever going to get through the process of interviewing someone about a subject that I was sure would put me to sleep, only to find that it was anything but that. Take risks. Learn about new things. You may be happily surprised to learn that the topics you know nothing about are your best assignments.

Early on in my freelancing days, I decided I wanted to write an article about whitewater rafting. This came some weeks after I experienced for myself the thrills of whitewater rafting on a river. I queried newspaper editors about doing such an article but got no takers. Finally, a travel editor for a major metropolitan newspaper told me to go ahead and write the article, although he couldn't guarantee his paper would use it. I went ahead and wrote it, despite no promise of publication or money. Weeks went by, and I heard nothing from that editor. Finally, one December day I peered into my mailbox to find a check for two hundred dollars from the newspaper.

I don't advise anyone to try and make a living writing exclusively for markets that offer no promise of return for your hard work otherwise known as writing on spec. I decided to write the whitewater rafting piece because I was jazzed up about the subject. I had a great time riding the rapids of that river, and the fun from that day translated to my writing. It was an easy piece to put together. I like to think the writing is what sold the article. As a matter of fact, I later sold the story to two other newspapers. All told, I made more than four hundred dollars from that article.

As you can see, you don't have to be an expert on a particular subject to write about it. I knew next to nothing about whitewater rafting but turned it into a published article that earned me money. You can do the same. The next time you go on vacation look around for ideas for freelance opportunities. What about that charming bed & breakfast you stayed in the last time you were in New England or along the Oregon coast? Perhaps there's a story there. Or how about that out-of-the way restaurant with the quirky menu items? Could be a story there.

Stories, articles are all around us, and people are eager to read them. Use the Internet and explore the world. And remember, you don't have to be an expert, a great writer to be a successful freelancer.

Turn single assignments into multiple articles. The whitewater rafting story is an example. But you can also rewrite articles you sold to single markets and sell them elsewhere. Or you can find a different angle from an assignment and write a completely different story for some other client.

Spend some time now and then just brainstorming for ideas. You might be surprised what ideas will come into your head by sitting on your front porch for ten minutes a day sipping at your morning coffee. Take walks around your community and look around. Stories are everywhere.

Inform your friends, your family, acquaintances that you are a freelance writer and open to suggestions for stories and eager for assignments. Networking is so important in any career. The more people you know the better.

Chapter 28

Let's say you been at this freelance career a few years now. You've tapped into some markets, found enough assignments to keep you fairly busy. The dollars are flowing in. Perhaps you've even quit the day job.

What now?

You might find it rewarding and fun to talk to others about this wonderful world of freelance writing. Perhaps you can contact the local community college about teaching a class on the subject. Share your wisdom, knowledge, and interesting experiences as a freelance writer. It's another means of getting your name out there, and it can be mean a few extra dollars.

Talk to local organizations about freelance writing. Plenty of groups are looking for speakers to address their meetings and functions. Sometimes you can earn fees. But even if the dollars don't come with speaking gigs, it's still a great way to promote your business.

Spread some goodwill. Join a local writers' group. Help a struggling writer. Many writers are timid souls who can't overcome the obstacle of getting started in some kind of writing career. Maybe you can steer a writer or two in the right direction. Kindly gestures are often reciprocated. But they can be their own reward as well.

Resumes, a Great Market for Freelance Writers

Chapter 29

I started writing resumes because I wanted to make a little bit of money. At the time, I was looking to see what was out there in the way of freelance writing possibilities. That was nearly fifteen years ago.

It was a good decision. Of all the freelance writing I've done over the years, doing resumes is probably the easiest gig out there. Why? People come to you. This shouldn't be surprising. People need jobs. Sure, there are plenty of people out of work in search of employment. But those are just some of the customers you can find for resume work.

Over the years, I've done resumes for folks who want to update an old resume and also for those who have never before had one. I've created resumes for college students, for retirees trying to re-enter the job market on a part-time basis. Of course, I've written my share of resumes for people who really need full-time jobs, but many also for those working and looking to change jobs or careers. Some people need resumes to apply for jobs within the company where they are already employed.

As you can see, all sorts of people need resumes. For most people, the whole job-search process can be a teeth-grinding ordeal. Most people are happy to hand off the task of writing a resume to someone else. That's where you, the resume writer, come in.

Do you want to pick up some extra cash writing resumes? Perhaps you're interested in writing resumes for a full-time income. Keep reading. You'll find some great information for learning how to get started writing resumes and plenty of other great insights from an experienced resume writer.

Chapter 30

Let's face it. The job market isn't like it used to be. There was a time when a person left high school or graduated college and took a job and often stayed with a particular company or organization for life. At the ripe old age of sixty-five or even before that, you retired, picked up a gold watch from a longtime employer to retreat to a life of leisure   the golf course, a boat, a gaggle of grandchildren.

We live in a different age today. Markets have changed. The economy is all so different now. People are switching jobs, starting new careers as never before. That's good news for people who want to write resumes.

Again, there are plenty of people who need resumes, and most of them don't want to do it themselves. It's probably safe to conclude that most people would rather submit to a root canal than go about the task of putting together their own resumes. But resumes aren't that hard to put together. You don't have to be great writer. You don't need any kind of special credentials to create resumes.

What is a resume?

To most people, a resume is a summary of one's skills and experiences, education and training targeted toward securing a job. But of course, it's more than that. A good resume successfully highlights a person's strengths and accomplishments. It's a job seeker's first line of attack, one might say, toward tackling the job market.

Sound competitive? Well, it is. The job market is competitive. You want to write resumes that make your clients stand out. Say a client, we'll call him Joe Doe, comes to you with a background in sales. How would you put together his resume? Better yet, how could you make the resume stand out and help convince a prospective employer to hire this person?

This is an easy one. Salespeople are valued for the sales they make. If I was hired by this client to write his resume, I'd want to know his sales figures for a given year or time period, and I'd get this very information into the resume. Therefore, if Joe Doe generated sales of $5.5 million for XYZ Company in 2019, I'd include those figures. Perhaps Joe Doe trained or managed people while working at XYZ Company. This too is vital information to put on the resume. It shows that Joe has leadership skills. Maybe Joe also came up with some unique idea that helped the company churn out even more sales. This brainstorm of Joe's could have been anything, from pinpointing a certain problem that was heretofore hurting the company to hiring a key person that helped business.

Do you see where we're going here? When you sit down with a person to write a resume, spend a little time searching for his or her strengths. Accentuate the positive. It doesn't take a whole lot of time. But it's time well spent.

Some of the important questions to consider for your resume clients are as follows:

* What specific job are you seeking?

* Are you changing jobs?

* What specific tasks have you carried out in your work history? How are they important for securing the job you want?

* How have you helped your companies or organizations for which you've worked succeed?

* Why are you the *best* candidate for the position?

These questions are vital for getting at the essence of a person's jobs skills and background. They are an important part of the interview process. Drill clients with these questions when you interview them. After you conduct a few interviews, you'll likely know these questions by heart.

Chapter 31

In the first chapter I went over the importance of highlighting clients' strengths and accomplishments and job skills. Let's take a look now at what a typical resume looks like.

There are a few basic different ways to write resumes. The most common one is what I call the professional resume which merely summarizes a person's job experiences in chronological order. This resume is for a person who has plenty of work experience. The best way to compose a professional resume is to list each of the past jobs pertinent to the job the client is seeking, starting with the most recent one.

Here is an example:

Zeke Zellers
43 N. Fourth St
Boonville, Fla.
Phone: 555-555-555
email: zellers136@service.org

Objective

To draw on my vast experience of award-winning reporting on events and stories toward assuming a leadership role in a newsgathering organization.

Work Experience

1999 to Present
Plum Gazette
Plum, Fla.
Reporter

* Successfully handle daily news gathering and writing responsibilities for this mid-sized daily newspaper.
* Write in-depth as well as breaking news stories, feature stories and other topics of community concern or interest.
* Help colleagues to develop stories to provide teamwork atmosphere in developing overall award-winning news product.
* Take part in planning sessions for daily operations.
* Structure and maintain records-keeping for successful day-to-day reporting needs.

1989 to 1997
Bilford Standard
Bilford, Fla.
Reporter

* Executed daily operations of news gathering and reporting for this award-winning community newspaper.
* Trained new reporters in news gathering and newsroom operations.
* Worked in collaboration with colleagues to develop daily product.
* Structured and maintained a data base of information for job needs.
* Provided valuable editing and proofreading skills to support staff.

Education

Sycamore College
Booneville, Fla.
Bachelor's Degree

Bilford Paramedic Training Institute
Bilford, Fla.
Paramedic Certification

Awards

Florida Press Association, First Place, Investigative
Reporting
United Press International, Honorable Mention, Feature
Reporting

References

Available upon request

As you can see, each of the jobs is listed with bullet points,
designating what duties and responsibilities were carried out. Notice
how many of the short descriptions include action verbs sometimes
with powerful adjectives or adverbs to accentuate the positive. For
example, he *structured and maintained* a data
base. He *successfully* handles news gathering. The resume indicates
he's trained people and helped colleagues develop stories. This
clearly shows he had a vital role with the company. He was not just
another worker drone, reporting to work, picking up a paycheck.
This person has been a valuable component to his employers. He's
described as performing his duties for award-winning newspapers. A
prospective employer will pick up on this.

When I meet with a client, I strive to bring out some of these
positive aspects of his or her work history. Don't get me wrong. I
don't encourage or ask anyone to fabricate anything. The point is
many people are hesitant about talking themselves up, of shining the
light on their accomplishments. Many other people forget about
some of the important contributions they made as employees.
Perhaps they trained a group of people or served in some strategic

position for a time but forgot about it. It could well be that they stepped up and all but ran a small company, if even briefly. Such information should be in a resume. Again, do not make up anything, but don't let a client shy away from accomplishments.

Now let's look at other parts of the resume.

The objective section under the job seeker's biographical information is an important aspect of any resume. This serves as a summary of what your client seeks in the way of employment. Let's refer once again to Joe Doe, the man with the sales background.

Perhaps Joe is looking to sell cars for a particular automobile dealership, the one with the dozen or so locations around the region. Joe would want to have his objective written in such a way that it targets that dealership. An example might be: *Looking to utilize my vast experience and award-winning automobile sales accomplishments to work for Good Deal Bill Cars and Trucks.*

This sends a clear message of what Joe Doe wants. Don't you think?

Let's look now at education. It's vitally important to include on the resume colleges and any special training, particularly if the job being sought demands certain educational requirements. Some jobs require unique skills but not necessarily college degrees.

Awards and special accomplishments strengthen a resume, especially if they are somehow pertinent to the job seeker's work experience or career. Again, many people can be hesitant about pounding their chests, but the inclusion of even one or two awards on a resume certainly makes the job candidate better stand out.

For references, a job seeker should list anyone who can attest to his or her upstanding character or excellent work history. I don't like to include any more than three, perhaps four people in the reference section along with their contact information. Ideally, they should be people that your client has worked with, preferably supervisors or managers. Many job seekers sometimes want to insert the names of friends or other people they've known through community organizations. For obvious reasons, listing relatives as references should be avoided.

Chapter 32

When I conduct interviews with clients, I prefer them to be face-to-face. I think this is the best approach for putting together their resumes and helping them land the job they want. Many people, as I mentioned earlier in the book, simply need to have an updated resume. Often, I get handed resumes that are not really resumes at all, but handwritten documents that include listings of past jobs, perhaps schools attended and other background stuff.

I've had clients provide me with reams of unnecessary information that they hope to somehow include in a resume. It's important to make it clear to a client that resumes should be no more than two pages. I've made exceptions to this rule. I once did a resume for a state government employee looking to secure another job within the agency for which he was already working. He insisted that we include each special skill and all training he had secured while employed there as well as all of the duties he'd performed, of which there were many. We went back and forth in emails and on the phone. I think I wrote three different resumes for him, each longer than the previous one.

There's an important lesson here. The customer comes first. Most clients will come to you for your expertise in writing resumes. It's possible you'll come across those who will insist it be done *their* way. You have the choice of throwing up your hands and writing the resume the way they want it done, or insisting it be done the way you see fit. Your job is to provide guidance and advice, and ultimately, to write the resume. How much time you want to spend going back and forth with that occasional difficult client is up to you. Just be advised that if you have a busy resume service, demanding and nitpicky clients can eat up a lot of your time. That might be fine if you charge by the hour, which I don't advise.

Most of the time, you'll get clients who get out of the way after the interview process and allow you to write the resume as you see fit. I always make it clear to clients that prospective employers don't want to wade through a lot of information. Quite often, they are busy people with other resumes to consider. Resumes should not be lengthy and cluttered with a lot of superfluous information.

Many job seekers want a resume targeting a specific job or single company. Perhaps the desired job was found on the internet or while scanning the classified ads of the local newspaper. If such is the case, the objective section of the resume can be written in a way as to specify how your client can help the company. The job descriptions will also target in on that very job.

If say, your client wants to get hired as a girls' basketball coach for a school, make it clear, if such is the case, that your client previously coached youth sports or girls. Perhaps, the client held jobs unrelated to coaching in which her or she assumed management or leadership roles. By querying a client, you can find those strengths, job skills or past experiences which can be used to best target the resume.

Many other people need resumes of a general nature. They aren't looking to narrow their job searches to a particular company or even a specific job. You may get a client with a very spotty job history that has included work as a counselor, a journalist, and a telemarketer. Of course, all these jobs require special skills, which can be highlighted in the job descriptions for the companies.

Let's say that Joe Doe held each of the aforementioned jobs over a ten-year period. As a counselor, he certainly had to have had interpersonal skills. He likely developed the ability to reach out to people and help them. As a journalist, he required similar skills as well as the ability to write and develop stories for readers from interviews and gathering information. Finally, as a telemarketer, he required some degree of proficiency in sales and some degree of interpersonal skills.

One might compose an objective in the resume that reads as follows: *To secure a job with XYZ company utilizing my writing and interpersonal skills successfully developed through my years working as a journalist, counselor, and salesperson.* The resume would successfully draw the attention of a prospective employer looking for someone who could perform any multitude of jobs that involve communicating with people.

In essence, a resume can be written with respect to an individual's particular experiences and skill levels. But beyond that, it can bring out the strengths of one's background and job history.

A college student with virtually no work experience but who hopes to land a job needs a much different type of resume. Here, it would be important to emphasize education and perhaps some of the job seeker's school or even volunteer activities. Educational information rather than work experience would come after the objective section of the resume. If the job seeker was an excellent student and attained a high grand point average, such information should certainly be included. But just as important, if not more so, are some of the activities related to the realm of study and the job your client seeks. Perhaps the client served as president of a campus business club or was involved in various charitable organizations.

For a recent college graduate looking to enter the job market, awards and activities need to be emphasized in a resume. Make sure such clients are not hesitant about listing some of these special and noteworthy accomplishments.

Chapter 33

We've looked at what to put in a resume, but what about what not to include. Sure, a resume should grab the attention of a prospective employer and hopefully lead to the offer of a job. It outlines the key components of a person's skills, accomplishments and work history and clearly states how a person can benefit a company or organization.

Include only important information on resume. Forget the personal stuff. Do not list on the resume that the job seeker is in good health or is married. Forget listing physical descriptions and the fact that he or she is one fantastic cook (unless of course the job being sought is preparing food in a restaurant).

Don't include photos of a person in a resume or cutesy designs and colors. There is perhaps no better way to doom a resume than to make it appear unprofessional. Don't create resumes on colored paper that can further lend it an unprofessional look. High quality white paper is best.

Always make sure the resume is free of mistakes. Run it through a spell check on the computer. Read it aloud to ensure it sounds right and doesn't contain problems. Hand it off to someone else to proofread. I can't stress enough the importance of having in place a resume that is free of errors. Remember, you were given a job to create a resume for someone in return for money. It's your responsibility to make the resume as good as it can be.

Now that I've brought up the subject of money, the question arises: How much should you charge for a resume? When I started writing resumes in 2007, I assessed clients a flat fee of fifty dollars. I felt it was fair at the time. Later, given the time and effort I was putting into each of the resumes, I felt I was underpricing my services. I later raised my costs to eighty dollars before eventually settling one hundred dollars per resume. That price includes the writing of a cover letter.

I think one hundred dollars is more than a fair price. If you live in an affluent community or an area where plenty of professional people reside, you may want to consider charging much higher prices. Assess your market. Who will be your clients? Professional people? Blue collar workers? College students? Chances are your clients will be a mix of different people looking for various jobs.

Let's break down exactly what I do for my one hundred dollars. Normally, when I'm contacted to do a resume, I set up an appointment to meet with the job seeker. I get to know this person just a little bit during this brief phone conversation. I like to find out what job is being sought or why a resume is needed. We agree on a time to meet, and I advise the job seeker to bring along any necessary information that will help in putting together the resume. If the client has an old resume, I suggest that it be brought to our meeting. At this meeting, I usually spend anywhere from a half hour to forty-five minutes having the client help me outline a rough draft of the resume. I ascertain if the client needs either a general resume or one of a more specific nature targeting certain work.

I work with the client to come up with an objective, what skills and experiences he or she brings to a prospective employer or the general job market. I try to encourage my clients to put forth a positive image in the resume. And of course, I do not under any circumstances encourage clients to falsify information or even lie about anything. Lies and falsehoods can only come back and hurt a client. Rarely, do these sessions with a client go beyond an hour.

Once I have the rough outline of the resume, I return to my home office and get it onto the computer. I use the same computer program for all my resumes. In many cases, the rough outline I sketched out with my client doesn't have to be greatly altered. I can usually find better ways to word certain aspects of the resume. I may add or delete some things. At any rate, this process of getting the resume onto the computer often takes no more than an hour.

So far, including the interview of my client, I've spent about one hour and forty-five minutes on a single resume. If the client wants a cover letter, and in most cases, they do, I proceed with that. I won't go into a lot of detail about how to compose cover letters. Suffice to say, cover letters are an introduction. Cover letters should never be more than one page. They let the prospective employer know the job candidate is interested in a job and how he or she can help the company. Cover letters usually should be no more than a few paragraphs.

Here is an example of the type of general cover letter I often do for clients.

William D. Blevins
220 Cooperstown Dr.
Cooperstown, N.Y. 17752
555-555-5555

March 24, 20201

Personnel Manager
Michelson & Son, Inc.
300 Howard St.
P.O. Box 248
Zellersville, Me.

Dear Personnel Manager:

In response to your recent advertisement, please accept this letter in application for the Copywriter/Proofreader position.

As you can see from my enclosed resume, my academic background, as well as my diverse skills in writing, editing and management make me a strong candidate for this position.

I would appreciate the opportunity to discuss my credentials with you at a mutually convenient time. Thank you for your consideration.

Respectfully yours,

William D. Blevins

Enclosure: Resume

As you can see, the cover letter is short with a clear message. Again, a cover letter is an introduction, an invitation, if you will, for the prospective employer to read the resume.

I often spend no more than fifteen minutes writing a cover letter. Up to now, I've spent about two hours on one client. Perhaps another ten minutes or so of time is needed for proofreading and making any necessary corrections to the resume and cover letter. If I hand the resume and cover letter off to someone else to look over, that may be another five or ten minutes.

After that, it's merely a process of sending off the resume and cover letter to the client by email. All told, I've worked somewhere between two and three hours for a single client. As you can probably see, a hundred-dollar fee for the amount of time and effort put into a single resume is certainly not out of line. Many resume writers charge more.

I inform clients that at any time they can ask me to alter the resume. That's one reason I like to email them the finished product. This allows us to send it back and forth, if necessary, and easily make any needed changes. Usually, I don't get asked to change anything. Sometimes I miss something that should have been included in the resume and we can work out the mistakes or needed changes through emails. I've rarely come across a client who has been dissatisfied with my services. The key to avoiding problems with clients is to keep the lines of communication open. Be diligent and always proofread your work.

Chapter 34

Where do you find prospective clients for your resume service? A great advantage of this type of business is that the clients come to you. It involves no door-to-door sales or telemarketing. In both bad and good economic times, people search for jobs and need resumes.

One of the easiest and cheapest ways to advertise your services as a resume writer is to make up flyers and brochures and hang them out on bulletin boards in high pedestrian traffic areas. Post offices, laundromats, supermarkets, convenience stores, and libraries nearly always have bulletin boards. Talk to the managers of these businesses or organizations and ask if you can place your advertisements there. The only cost here is the price of paper for churning out the materials on your home computer. Of course, you can get fancy too. Hiring a professional to print up glossy advertisements that really stand out will cost you money, but it will most surely attract more clients. Don't just hang up your advertisements at a few locations and be done with it. Print up dozens of brochures and flyers around your community to get the attention of plenty of people.

Use business cards to advertise your services. Business cards are cheap to create. Print your own or find a printer in your community or over the internet to do them for you. Pin them on the same bulletin boards with your flyers and brochures. Hand your cards out to friends, family and acquaintances. Let them know you're a resume writer and are actively seeking clients.

Consider joining a community organization or two, preferably one you'd like be involved with. Such groups are everywhere and a means of networking with people and getting your name out there. It's also a great way to meet new people and form friendships and business acquaintances.

Years ago, I advertised the yellow pages and clients found my ad under *Resume Services*. Admittedly, people use the yellow pages less and less these days, but they still draw customers. Consider taking out a classified ad in the jobs section of the local newspaper or the newspaper online edition. Believe it or not, people still read the newspaper, many of them just to check the classifieds for jobs.

The internet, of course, offers all sorts of possibilities for advertising. Consider putting up a website advertising your services. There's Facebook, Twitter and LinkedIn and other social network sites to consider.

Attend job fairs. Set up a booth and make yourself available to people who stop by. People either looking to change jobs or enter the workforce flock to job fairs. Renting space as a vendor at a job fair usually costs a little bit of money, but the price can often be exceeded by the clients you find. Job fairs are happening all the time. Check out the internet to find one close where you live.

Is there a college, technical school, or other institution of higher learning in or near your community? Students are some of the best clients for resume writers, especially those in their final year of study looking to hit the job market. They desperately need resumes.

Make a visit to the school. Introduce yourself to school officials. Let it be known you write resumes. Consider offering discounts of your services to students. It's a great way to get a foot in the door with the school. With time you can find more clients there.

Visit employment offices in your area. Get to know some of those people. The key is to get your name out there. Let people know you have a valuable service to offer. Initially, you may not find a lot of clients at schools and unemployment offices. Don't get discouraged. You're planting seeds, and those seeds can lead to future growth for your services.

Contact local newspapers. The business sections of newspapers need to fill space. Have a press release done or write your own and get it to the editor of the business section. Newspapers run press releases free of charge. Just getting news of your business in the newspaper is a big plus. Perhaps the newspaper runs special features on its business page about new businesses. Don't be shy about talking to a reporter and being interviewed about your business. Again, this is a no-cost option.

How about radio? Stations run public service announcements including those for businesses, and they are free of charge. Just as newspapers have space to fill, radio has airtime it must fill. Check the commercial stations in your local community, but also the college stations as well. Remember, college students are some of the best sources for resumes.

Of course, there is still the old word of mouth advertising. The key here is to always do a good job writing resumes. Be courteous, respectful of your clients. People happy with the job you do, with the way you treat them, will often reward you with referrals.

Consider talking about your resume service to groups or organizations. If you don't mind public speaking, this can be a great way to connect your business to people. Conduct a brief presentation on resume writing. People love to learn how to do something of value. Don't look at it as giving away your services for free. Many of the people will instead remember that you're a resume writer and perhaps later contact you or tell others about your services.

Draw new clients with enticements. Offer special discounts during certain times of the year. Reduce your rates for students or veterans or other prospective clients who fall in special categories. Hand out pens or other trinkets to clients bearing the address, website or email of your resume business. People love to get things for free, and your information on that pen or other gift will serve as a reminder to them of the service you offered them and perhaps draw the interest of others who see it. Beyond that, the gifts can convey the message that you are a professional with a business.

I would highly discourage spending a lot of money upfront for advertising, especially if you don't have a lot of money. You don't want to dig yourself in a financial hole before your business is barely off the ground. Try some of the low-cost advertising initially. See how it goes. Don't put all your eggs in one basket. Maybe social media is all you really need to do initially. The point is not to get discouraged. It takes time to build up any business.

Chapter 35

Let's say you've been at this business of writing resumes for a while now. You've found clients, begun to build your business. Perhaps you're even thinking about quitting that day job that's been stopping you from doing what you really want to do: becoming a full-time resume writer. Maybe it's time to think long-term.

Get proactive. How about all those clients for whom you've written resumes? Perhaps each of them knows one or two people who can benefit from your services. Hopefully, you've kept the emails or other contact information of former clients. Contact them and find out how their job searches came out. Did the resumes you wrote for them help? If so, maybe they have a referral or two for you. Ask former clients if they can write a one or two sentence testimonial of the valuable service you provided them. Include the testimonials on your flyers, brochures or other advertising you do.

Keep abreast of what's happening in your community. Maybe a local company is furloughing people. That can mean people suddenly without jobs and perhaps needing resumes to find other work. Maybe you know some of these people. Contact them. Perhaps you can offer to do their resumes at reduced prices. Companies often offer training to former employees they cut loose. Perhaps you can contact the company and work out a deal whereby you provide resume training for these out-of-work people.

Whether you decide to be a part-time or full-time resume writer, it's most important that you provide the best service possible for your clients. People need jobs to live and to put a roof over their heads and to feed their families. They deserve your best effort, and the better job you do for clients only increases your chances of success.

Have fun.

The End

To find other books by Mike Reuther, check out his author
page: http://www.amazon.com/Mike-Reuther/e/B009M5GVUW.